AF593401

Just Deserts

in two parts

A collection of poetry by Anne Arasin

Contents

Part I

Part I

Sacramento, 2015 – 2016

On the toxicity of daffodils

Wikipedia describes it as low but recommends
calling poison control if ingested.
That's not what my mom did when her 7-year-old
daughter ate daffodils.

I pulled them up from my neighbor's garden
before church and kept their bulbs in my pocket,
nibbling away at the smooth, green pods
as my Sunday school teacher discussed Jesus

feeding bread and fish to his disciples.
Baskets never emptying.

They tasted bitter, but I persisted. I offered
my teacher a handful, which she declined,
instead suggesting that I pray for non-Christians.
We got home and I ran to the bathroom.

I couldn't stop vomiting until Thursday
when my parents threatened to take me to the ER
if I didn't eat. Through sheer force of will,
I ate the plate of brown rice they presented me.

I'd only been to the hospital once when I split
open my knee playing in the backyard.

The doctor sewed me up with no anesthetic
that I remember and no smile. Not wanting
to relive the experience, I healed myself.
Ever since, I haven't believed in grownups.

Withering

One night in July, I needed a break from packing
and went for a walk. I came across an abandoned
cactus stand. Several cacti stood, patient,
waiting for customers. A sign leaning against
the stand read, "Pay what you want." I put down
$10 and took two home.

When we moved to Boston three weeks later,
I left them in the care of my mother-in-law,
who never mentioned them again.

Now, we're in California, and I can't keep
a cactus alive. I wander through the streets,
and cacti wither as I go. I'm Maleficent, burning
under the persistent sun. My skin peels away
to reveal more pale skin.
I don't belong.

Accordion

Driving to Davis today, I couldn't stop looking at birds
pulsing in the air. They were almost like a wave
crashing into rock and sand, knocking people
over with a bubbly laugh.

Birds can't knock anything over. Even the clouds
don't give way to them. They're completely malleable
against the gray sky, an accordion gliding across
the rainy horizon.

As I watched, a crow launched itself
from a telephone line and beat its wings, frantic,
fighting the competing gust to join the flock
higher up. I don't know if she made it.

Flurries

The thought of California snow brings to mind
that scene from *Father of the Bride*: Steve Martin
playing basketball with his daughter in their driveway
the night before her wedding. Bathrobes
and sneakers. Such intimacy.

I've only been here a year, but it hasn't snowed
in over two decades. "We got some flurries
when I was a kid once," a friend tells me. "We all ran
to the window at school and watched for half an hour."
"Half an hour?" I say, surprised.

But even the rain makes me pause these days.
I don't own boots anymore.
They haven't been missed.

My dad's younger sister

Her eulogy was sandwiched between
an Angry Birds invitation
and Donald Trump's head
superimposed on Dolores Umbridge.
My husband's phone rings,
but I already know who it is
since I woke up to Facebook.

"Your mom only calls me when somebody's died."
This time, it's my aunt. 57. "Is there something
we can do to commemorate her?" He only met her
once. He doesn't know how loud her laugh was,
and sometimes cruel. He never saw her bracelets
jangle on her wrists, the turquoise stones
she always wore.

I never told him how she bought herself fur-lined
clogs when they found my grandpa's body
on the floor, stiff with hours of death,
reaching for the ceiling.
Her second husband was the kindest man
I ever met. He loved fireworks and was killed
by cancer soon after their wedding.

I didn't visit him before he died.
I avoid the dying when possible—
their faces either swollen or haggard beyond
recognition. Three thousand miles away
and I can still feel the lack of her.

17

I went to bed one night when I was 17,
leaving my dad in the kitchen in a drunken stupor,
black pork chops sizzling in a pan on the stove.
The first floor was engulfed in smoke
before the alarm went off.

I imagine my mom woke up, ran downstairs,
and threw the pan into the sink. It probably hissed
and produced another cloud of acrid pork and onions.
I imagine my dad woke up, not remembering,
having nothing to apologize for.

Night terrors

When I can't sleep, I imagine laying
in a hammock on the beach. My fingers drag
across the hot sand, scattering hermit crabs.

The quick rhythm of their scuttling legs lulls me.
Are hermit crabs heavy enough to generate
footsteps? In place of counting sheep,

they'll have to do.

I don't even like the beach. Or the sun. I'm at home
on a cloudy day with orange leaves fluttering
to the ground. Or even dropping at a steady pace,

weighed down by rain and anticipation of winter.

Winter never comes here. And the leaves
are a dry brown. But at least I can imagine
a cool breeze on my skin to offset the sun.

New fruit

The ground is littered with citrus every spring.
Trees throw down lemons and limes, disgusted
when they realize acid doesn't mix well with anything.

During our third week of dating, my ex took me
to Philadelphia. We ordered chocolate-covered
strawberries with milk and pranced around the hotel
room in animal print robes.

I donned the giraffe. He took the tiger. We played
Monopoly until 3 a.m. That morning,
I was mesmerized by his teeth-brushing routine.
He caught my eye in the mirror and asked
what I was staring at.

Now, ~~we~~ I have a plum tree. ~~We're~~ I'm drowning
in plums. I take bags of them to work. Sometimes
they're already rotten and drip all over
the break room counter.

Blues

A stroke stole the laugh lines from my grandpa's
eyes, which were the clearest, crispest things
I'd ever seen. Cerulean even. Most of my family
has blue eyes. But his were the brightest.

The blue eyes on my dad's side are more gray—
zapped of all color—perhaps the first time
his mom finished three bottles of wine at lunch—
perhaps the first time his dad beat him
for eating with his elbows on the table.

No, my dad's eyes are not cerulean. They're more
like the color of DMV tiles. They're my eyes too.
Maybe we just evoke a feeling of lifelessness
from generations of cold parenting.

My mom's eyes are hazel and watery.
Maybe she imagined cerulean in my dad's eyes
in the beginning since they were blue, not realizing
there are different blues. She thought they were eyes
she could take root in.

But tile doesn't give way to roots.
I've digressed. My grandpa's eyes were blue.
After his stroke he rarely laughed. But he did request
pancakes for breakfast every morning.

On the taste of metal

or maybe the smell of metal—
I consider it desert foliage
since the leaves are all dead here.
Not dead from fall, just dry, mummified
by the worst drought California's ever seen.

We're left with forests of cars,
their skin emitting that sweet, tangy scent,
like after you've handled coins—
which smell like every person
they've ever touched.

Metal manages to be clean and dirty all at once.
You can feel it on your fingertips, a thin layer
of heat, palpable. You shake someone's hand
and the metal transfers from your palm to theirs,
hanging in the air before they walk away.

Later, they may rub their eyes, which will sting
a little, tear up. They'll have the sudden impulse
to bathe. The metal could remain for days,
producing sweat and spreading until everything
they own is contaminated.

Bovine

I have low tolerance for nipple pain.
These days, corporations have whole rooms
dedicated to pumping milk.

I imagine a group of young professionals
sitting in a circle, silent but for the steady drone
of breasts being sucked dry.

Maybe the sound of suction is broken up
by milk drip, dripping into a communal bucket or
the occasional tap of a stiletto.

From crazy
After Barbara Kopple's *Running from Crazy*

Crazy is personified in my mind.
It's persistent, a steady jog, running
through my family like boiling water,
scalding the inside of our veins
until they're pink and unrecognizable.

The Hemingways have been running
from crazy for years. Dad retreated
to his basement. Muffet was carted away.
Suicide became enticing.
Familial.

My family and I haven't graced Vogue,
but we're forgeries of ourselves—our curls,
our stuck-up noses, our gray eyes
(usually portrayed as romantic in literature,
but really they lack warmth, color, personality).

We're more like a clan of zombies than humans—
branded by a legacy that propels us farther
from each other and into dangerous ideas
(like the best way to remove eyes
from a breathing body).

In Equus, the horses' eyes are stabbed
out. Among us, it's our own eyes
we can't stand. Two poinsettias
blooming from our cheekbones.
I've been running so long

I don't recognize my surroundings.
Dust, dying trees, brown grass, and cacti.
These artfully placed cacti don't wave

or blossom. They just stand, complacent,
ready for a thorny embrace.

Crazy overflows onto the desert sand,
sizzling, dissipating in the clean air.
But that burning scent lingers.

Diaspora

"Are those stigmata on your baby?"
one woman asks another, who's breastfeeding
at the gynecologist. I imagine they're strangers
even though you don't sit next to a stranger
at the gynecologist.

You don't sit next to a stranger when
they're breastfeeding. You don't sit next to a loved
one when you're breastfeeding.
Having your nipples sucked requires a certain
sense of privacy.

You don't even have to look your baby in the eyes
as it slurps away at you. The breastfeeding woman
looks up with a sheepish grin on her face
because she's an atheist but still understands
the implications of stigmata.

She comes from Catholics. I recognize
my own even in my most displaced state.

Our hospitality

How long does it take to get glass out of carpet?
I broke a glass yesterday. Then, I vacuumed
for two hours. To be safe, I did laps around
the coffee table in my bare feet.

"Better me than someone else," I thought,
pulling invisible pieces out of my skin,
wiping away the blood.

It reminds me of Sodom and Gomorrah.
Biblical scholars will tell you
that cautionary tale is not about sodomy,
but the consequences of inhospitality.

"Please, rape my daughter, not these poor Angels
who have been traveling all day, who missed
their connection in Denver.

Let them eat fish and bread. If they want,
they can drink from me, so much thicker
than wine, so much more substantive
than those little bags of peanuts

and the half-can of Coke poured over ice
with a hint of grit, a touch of crunch
that doesn't melt away."

Buddhism

There's a species of lizard that has evolved
to reproduce asexually. If there were no men,
who would kill the spiders?

We're a progressive couple.
My husband is generally against killing,
a policy that I used to respect.

But one night, I trapped a spider under a glass
and carried it down three stories to let it outside.
As I opened the front door, I dropped the glass.

It broke and killed the spider.
I took that as a sign of divine intervention
and have been killing spiders ever since.

I don't understand his Buddhist attitude.
In Boston, we used to wake up to cockroaches
crawling on our bare backs.

To me, such an intrusion warrants the death penalty.
Unpacking boxes after our move to Sacramento,
we uncovered many cockroach carcasses

tucked between our books and utensils.
They were just little stowaways trying
to get to California.

Nice people

I got hit by a car once, and the culprit
offered to drive me home. She wore red pumps
and sobbed at my dining room table

as she wrote out her insurance information.
I told her not to worry. “We’re nice people.”
She looked like she wanted to scream.

Later, at Complete Care, The Cranberries
came on the radio while the doctor set my finger.
All I could see were red shoes.

Growth

My mom scattered plastic plants
around my house when I was growing up.
The dust they collected
sticks to my mind.

Spraying fake leaves with Pledge is pretty
bleak. That's why I bought three live cacti
for my first apartment
and promptly killed them from neglect.

I also have two stalks of bamboo
that refuse to die. When my mom came to visit,
she reminded me to water them.

Personification

Even a treadmill requires a sense of place.
You can't just shove her into the corner
of your bedroom and expect her to be okay.

They're like orcas in that way, set aside
in a windowless tank at the end of the day,
able to hear each other's lonely cries

but unable to see each other, to confirm
someone else is experiencing the same pain.
Inevitably, a trainer will get their arm bitten off

when she lashes out. I expect the treadmill
to snap her belt any day. I'll go flying
into my glass closet doors.

It will take forever to clean up the mess.

The antihero

I can't stop watching ballet documentaries—
how the dancers bend forward to touch the floor
with no effort or grimace of pain, their feet warped
from quarter-sized blister and bruises, calluses on top
of calluses on top of toes that don't look like toes
anymore. How does a person leap into the air
with a fractured tibia? What is a tibia? They're both
aggressive and graceful, up before the city stirs,
before the stars have sunk back into the night.

Meanwhile, I'm irredeemable in my own story.
Shoulders slumped, I lope through crowds,
avoiding eye contact with strangers.

#matriarchy

I'm at Target. "How tall are you?" a woman asks.
"You're taller than me. I need that root beer
on the top shelf."

I hand it to her. "Do you just need one?"
"No, I need two." I can't reach the second one
and apologize.

"It's okay, I'll make a man do it.
He hasn't done anything all day."
I laugh and walk away.

In line for Star Wars later that night,
My husband is telling me about video games.
The man ahead of us turns around in a way

that suggests confrontation. "I'm tired of know-it-all
hipsters trying to impress their girlfriends
with things they know nothing about."

"This is my wife," my husband counters.
"I stopped trying to impress her a long time ago."

Familiar

Some shed lovers like they shed eyelashes—
all over the coffee table.

If you press down on them with your index finger,
they stick to you.

Then, you can blow them and make a wish.
You can pull them out

one by one in times of anxiety and rub them off
against your jeans.

Or maybe they're scattered across your keyboard,
in the crevices,

waiting for a Clorox wipe. I don't like the warmth
of other people.

Blurred lines

I'm on a beach—the first clue that I'm asleep.
A man in a Kabuki mask steals my baby.
I fling the culprit into the air with my telekinesis.
As he floats towards space, I remove his limbs one
by one until he is a digit-less torso cursing my name.

Then, I release him, and he falls to the ground,
sending up a plume of sand. A screaming crowd
gathers in terror. I casually turn and head
towards the parking lot. I begin to run and transform
into a polar bear. But to be inconspicuous,

I make my fur fade to brown. Is a brown bear fleeing
the scene of a telekinetic crime less conspicuous
than a white bear? I catch my reflection
in a car's gleaming door—broad shoulders, pale skin,
a blank expression,

only now realizing I left my baby at 35,000 feet.

Running

I've been told I don't lift my legs enough.
And my feet stick out at odd angles.
I focus on my breath instead of form.
In three. Out two.

It's mid-February and everything's in bloom.
Sidewalks are littered with petals
and small yellow meadows line the pavement.
Straight out of *Anne of Green Gables*.

Were there meadows in *Anne of Green Gables*?
Were there sidewalks? At 6 a.m., when the sky's
still navy and there are no street lights,
everything's seeped in sepia.

Even an 11-year-old with a Spider-Man backpack
seems dangerous.

Groceries
After Rodrigo Garcia's *Nine Lives*

As I ponder tofu dogs, Robin Wright
wanders the aisles, flip flops smacking
in time to her squeaky cart.

I want to take her hand
so she can lead me to checkout,
but her fingers slip past mine.

That night, I grate my skin
over the chicken instead of Parmesan
and serve it to my husband.

My bloody stump
of a hand I hide behind my back
like a weapon. Or a surprise.

Crowds

I'm a fish. My scales flake off from beating rays
of California sun. My body flops on pavement.
My mouth gapes, shaping words I can't pronounce.
My eyes don't blink anymore, and I'm left to stare

up at the crowds as they bustle by, not noticing me,
not aware of my heart thumping every time
their shoe soles brush me to the side,
a little closer to the edge of the sidewalk.

Before, I was merely ornamental.
You could admire the bubbles floating out of my gills.
You could admire my rocks' reflective nature, admire
how they shimmered under the fluorescent tank light,

that precise shade of blue that burns if you consider
it too long, almost white, striking a balance
between warm and cold. If you tapped on the glass,
I'd float from side to side to side, looking startled.

Under your stern gaze, your persistent tapping finger,
I couldn't remember what I was doing 30 seconds
before. I couldn't remember if I'd already drifted
to the left for your amusement.

The barista asks me for my order. I say, "Tea.
Whatever you recommend. Whatever."
I just want to feel something hot in my throat.
The water in my bowl was chilly and stagnant.

But I had to keep swallowing to stay alive.
I still might end up rolling into a cul-de-sac.
But there's hope for the open ocean, currents
I can take or avoid, crowds of my own kind.

Birthday

September in Sacramento's not the autumn
of my childhood.

I'd like the leaves to be changing from changing
seasons, not from their waning will to live.

They crunch on the ground when you step on them,
a sound not reminiscent of crisp air or hard cider,

but of sunburn, sweat-slicked undershirts
sticking to your back as you breathe in fire.

All I want is a reason to wear long sleeves.

Crickets

There's a cricket infestation at work.
As a result, I've been jumping out of sleep at night,
screaming, the covers covered in insects.
My husband thinks I'm crazy but smacks the sheets

to placate me before putting me back to bed.
I'm suffering from phantom bugs crawling
on my body. Like phantom limbs. Except the crickets
are still out there, hopping from cube to cube,

not tempted by the boxes of poison
we've placed strategically near the doors.
One coworker's resorted to afternoon naps in his car
to sweat out his anxiety. I imagine him

with the windows rolled up,
breaths labored, drifting into a REM cycle.
Jolted awake by his alarm set to go off
every 10 minutes. Seatbelt on.

Architecture

Students are sitting at the table across from me
with a stencil paper spread. They're measuring out
steeples in intricate patterns. I wouldn't design

a church in a coffee shop. Too much caffeine.
Churches should be designed in nursing homes
where people remember what God feels like.

Hot

I find words of affection
difficult to express. But

there's something satisfying
about seeing someone sweat
through a button-down shirt.
Sometimes the sweat marks
look like faces…distant eyes
averted to the side and a mouth
stuck in an expanding frown.

Eventually, the pattern's lost
in a blotch of darkness, no longer
resembling sweat, just a purposeful
design. Usually, these strangers have
distinct, filmy scents. The smell
of skin cells. Organic, warm, salty.
The kind that makes you rub your eyes.

Paranoid personality disorder

Renowned hit man Richard Kuklinski
once hanged a man to avenge himself—
threw him over his shoulder with a rope
around his neck and held him until he
stopped kicking. I don't think I have
the upper body strength for such an act.
I'm not really one for vengeance either.
Though I do have many nemeses.

Endorphins

At the gym, I watch *Grey's Anatomy* reruns
and cry when teenagers pull the plug on their parents.

Tears and cardio lead to hyperventilating. So I count
my breaths. In in in out out. And repeat.

Watch Patrick Dempsey cut into a left hemisphere,
weepy eyes, frown obscured by his surgical mask.

Watch Ellen Pompeo reminisce
about merry-go-rounds

and contemplate drowning herself
in her mother's claw foot tub.

Belonging

You make a grand entrance,
your beret matching your pumps.
You place your order in Italian

and the barista stares, not comprehending.
You are the kind of person that orders
foreign coffee in foreign languages,

then answers your phone in American.
You offer to buy the barista a drink,
knowing he'll say yes but he shakes his head.

"I get them for free." You've both
romanticized this man and dismissed him.
Still on the phone. Still in a smooth California accent.

We are cut from different cloths. I'm only
now realizing people that don't flirt with baristas
are my people.

13

I'm sitting in a therapist waiting room with my sister.
I'm 13 and she's 10. My dad peed on my hamster
last week.

I saw his shadow stumble up the stairs
and followed him, suspicious. He was standing,
facing the wall in my bedroom.

I could hear the splash of urine and knew
I'd have to clean up in the morning. Pee is louder
than other liquids. Like it knows it doesn't belong.

He finished, zipped, then collapsed
in my bed, snoring. I walked into the room,
expecting a puddle on the floor.

Instead, my hamster's loud squeaks alerted me.
Her cage was drenched. She was frantically
wiping her face with her paws,

maybe not aware of the filth covering her.
I woke my mom up. She had me write a letter
to my dad about my feelings.

My feelings about a grown man peeing
on my hamster. A week later, my sister and I
are sitting in a therapist waiting room,

waiting to be summoned by my parents.
We play a game, sneaking up to the closed door,
trying to hear. I imagine my dad slumped over,

crying, or maybe just staring out the window,
saying nothing. They're in there for over an hour.

Then, we leave.

My question of why we weren't allowed inside
goes unanswered. "He peed on your hamster?"
my husband asks when I tell the story.

"You have to be so drunk to reach that point."
"I know." "You have to be so, so drunk for that,
like piss-your-pants drunk."

I get a flash—
a pile of laundry in the basement, jeans
with a stained crotch. "I know."

Belonging II

The other night, I was being held hostage
by rabid raccoons. They stared at me, eyes wide,
mouths foaming, steps rigid and sure.

My reflection in the glass was pregnant. Death stood
behind me, a frown under his hood.
The next morning, I woke with the comfort

that (for now) my body is my own.
I reach over to brush a strand of hair out of your eyes
and you lean away.

My smile drops.
Small rejections
cause little fissures.

My mother-in-law traveled abroad
and brought me back some tea from London.
I displayed the box on my desk at work,

drinking it with no milk, no sugar.
My experience: authentic.
Then I saw a display of the same tea

at CVS. I was buying tampons.
The next day I added Splenda
to my morning brew.

Renaissance man

The baker down the street is also a bounty hunter.
He stands alert in the middle of his store,
one hand behind his back, a fly swatter clenched
in a fist at his side, ready but unimposing.

The “slap” pause “slap” pattern permeates the air.
He pretends to watch TV behind the counter,
a ruse to lure in unsuspecting victims.

One day, I’ll order my chocolate muffin and a fly
will land on my head. Will the baker give me
my pastry or smack me with his swatter, let out
a triumphant war cry, and leave twitching legs

in my hair?

The female gaze

There's a cow standing
at the foot of my bed. Stripes of light
are filtering through the blinds.

She's staring, not blinking, swatting flies
with her tail. But there aren't flies in our apartment,
so her tail must be flicking out of habit.

Her eyes are very blank and very big.
She reads the doubt in my face and snorts.
Phantom cow boogers fly onto my comforter.

She snorts again and I can hear the wetness
of the snort even if I can't see it. Why is she staring
at me like she knows what I'm thinking?

Her udder swings between her legs.
I can just make out a small forest of pink nipples
illuminated in the dim sunlight.

She catches me staring at her bareness and frowns,
bends her neck forward, opens her mouth,
and grabs the corner of my comforter with her teeth.

Holding my gaze, she pulls her head back,
taking my bedding with her and exposing my legs.
I haven't shaved. I'm wearing only my underwear,

which has bled through the sheets
and into the mattress. I can tell from the way the red
pools through the cheap thread count.

Nowhere to go.

Andy Warhol

Downtown is abandoned.
It's 104 degrees. I can feel it
through the glass. As usual,
I'm an observer. A California girl
interviews a photographer.

"I started a blog because
there's an audience for what I do."
She uncrosses and recrosses her legs.
"Me on a Sunday, drinking
my coffee: story." "Boom."

He holds up his hands, framing
her in a picture he's taken
in his mind, then whips out
his portfolio to peruse
his own black and whites.

Part II

Central + South America, 2018 – 2019

Volcanoes

"Do you know the names of the volcanoes yet?"
my cab driver asks. He's in the middle of charging
me two soles too many to get home but I humor him,
"I know Misti, but not the others." He laughs
the laugh of a local who both loves and takes
for granted the Andes around him. I laugh with him,
the laugh of a tourist who longs to take volcanoes
for granted.

Down the street is an entire museum paying
homage to Incan sacrifice, Juanita, killed to keep
the volcanoes happy. Her tiny body was unearthed
after seismic activity, and they keep her frozen
for tourists to press their faces against her cold,
glass tomb. The exhibit ends with a to-scale
display of my town, rings of red, orange, and yellow
indicating whether, in the event of an eruption, I'll die.

(I'm two blocks away from harm, apparently.)

When I tell my dad I'm moving to Peru, he warns me
about the volcanoes. "If something goes wrong there,
Dad won't be there to help." He pauses, then says
my thoughts like he's read them, "Not that I've been
there lately anyway." A few months later,
he messages me without context, "How is Peru
for earthquakes?" "We had a small one the other
day," I tell him, "but I slept through it."

I don't tell him I thought it was a truck driving
down the road. Traffic is three feet from my head
at any given time, just on the other side of the wall
(a wall made from volcanic rock that crumbles
in my hair). He segues into a conversation

about my sister, who's made the time to visit my aunt
before she dies of cancer. The guilt is implicit,
but it rolls off me like lava.

The worst thing

I've been in Peru for two months and can barely
order a sandwich.

One of my students wrote an essay
about her girlfriend moving to France.
I'm not actively seeking out signs of the subversive,
but I long for them regardless.

I go out of my way to tell my students
that I'm divorced.

In a country where 90% of the population is Catholic,
that's just looking for trouble. My roommates take me
out to dinner for my birthday. Our landlord
discovers my marital status.

"I'm going to give you so much shit now," she says.
"Why?" I laugh. "I can't think of anything worse

than being divorced."
She is going to school and working two jobs
to support her family back home.
And divorce is worse.

Second deserts

Michael Myers is peering at me over the bathroom
stall wall. (In this production, the role
of Michael Myers will be played by Jonah Hill.)
He feels so far away. I can't even make out
his eyes behind the mask.

The eye holes are cast in shadow by fluorescents
tinged in yellow for the illusion of warmth.
But all they accomplish is an alien hue
on his pasty complexion, once so familiar. He wants
to extend a giant hand and touch my shoulder. I think.

His mouth is set in the same grim line, but
his breathing pattern betrays a desire to comfort.
I don't think his arms can extend enough to reach me
on the floor. I'm tired of heat, and these tiles are so
cool on my skin.

I exchanged one desert for another, though this one
is rife with metaphor in place of cacti. Sitting
in a crowded restaurant, my skin gathers dust,
and no one will look at me. I wait, patient, expecting,
until I'm just a pile of ground Andes.

The abuelita sweeps me into the street, rinses me
away with her mop water. Lonely bathroom tiles,
however gritty, are preferable to such a fate.
And I would take his distant gaze, longing
but unattainable, over their aversion.

Sick

"Everyone gets salmonella
from this kitchen at least once,"
one roommate warns me
the first time we meet,
incidentally, in the kitchen.

There are 15 of us in this hostel,
so I buy my own sponge and dish soap.
Several stomach bugs later,
someone suggests we be sexy cops
for Halloween.

Sustenance

I'm not having a good month. October is usually
my favorite time of year. Orange leaves, comfy
clothes, cuddling up with a pumpkin ale
and a scary movie. I have none of these things here.

I think I could handle the suffocating alienation
of living abroad if I could just watch *Halloween*
under three blankets, a cold, spicy beer in my hand.

I haven't been running. I laugh off my depressive
lethargy with my friends. My boyfriend is in California,
and I can't talk to him about it. There's never
a good time to bring anything up.

He has his own dreams to pursue. He can't hold
my hand as I stumble, reluctant, through my own
adventure. I hesitate even sending him a picture

of an Oreo milkshake. "No, it's ok, you don't have
to respond," I want to cut him off when I see
those throbbing ellipses pop up on my screen.
Milkshakes don't warrant anything

more than your passing attention.
I just wanted you to know that I left
my room today.

The WiFi is out at my hostel. The loss
of that small comfort sends my heart racing.
After morning classes, I go shopping
for Halloween decorations to lift my mood.

I march through traffic to the beat of constant honking
so common in Arequipa, bus pollution blowing

in my face, street dogs that growl at me, hardened.

I am undeterred. This is my every day. Party stores
line the streets near the mercado. Their shelves
are stocked with candy I don't recognize, Avengers
masks, flimsy witch hats.

What I wouldn't give for a Reese's
peanut butter cup right now. I settle on a bag
of cobwebs and a glow-in-the-dark skeleton.

My dad asks, "Do you feel successful there?"
Last Sunday, I sat in my hostel's yard in the shade,
getting drunk off a Cusqueña Marzen and a stack
of honey mustard Pringles,

researching beer school programs. One roommate
and coworker, a woman in her 70s who's been
traipsing through South America for two decades,

walked by and said, "I've been watching you
drinking beer, eating chips, reading.
You seem so sure of yourself, so self-sufficient,
it's nice to see."

Haunted

I can feel shadows watching me. They go out
of their way to stalk me through los baños
(enviably deep pools now empty), la cocina
(scorched black even after centuries of disuse),
las habitaciones (nun mattresses
evoke their own pain).

There's a fountain, green with algae,
possibly intentional, to offset los paredes rojos.
Me llena con una tristeza tan fondo que no puedo
respirar, este monasterio maldito.
Días y días después.

Fish swim through the algae, though one is dead.
It floats on the surface, still gleaming.
Muerte no puede parer la luz.
Pero el confesionario is the worst.

White walls go dark once the door is closed.
A small metal grate to receive your secrets. A bench
carved with stone. Unforgiving. Unforgivable.

I can't stop crying after I leave. Maybe this is
what happens when an atheist goes to a holy place.

God is spiteful, this much I know.

Cities

I don't like city living. On my way back from work
yesterday, a stranger shouldered past me,
almost knocking me to the pavement. I cried
when I got to my hostel. I don't want to be
here anymore. I don't want to be another face
in a sea of strangers, dodging cars
between traffic lights, buying candy from carts
on the street, expecting to be mugged. Like one
roommate who walked away with a bloody lip
and bruises, saving her cell phone by hiding it in
her front pocket, like another who was targeted
at an ATM because his six-year-old son was with him,
like a student who lost her laptop but kept her life
at gunpoint just a couple blocks from school.
I've stopped running.

Every time I turn a corner, my heart races at what
could be waiting for me. My favorite alleys
have grown menacing, places to avoid at twilight.
A shame really, since they have the best views
of Misti, Chachani, the sun hitting them
at such an angle that their peaks turn coral against
a periwinkle sky, perfectly cloudless. Perfect.
Someone asked me for directions yesterday, a tourist,
probably German. She wanted the best view
of the mountains and I told her about Puente de Grau,
neglecting to mention the growling dogs,
the bus drivers out for blood, the clouds
of exhaust blowing against the wind,
but also the warm cinnamon churros, the fedoras
and bowler hats for sale in neat rows
on the sidewalk, the gangs of laughing teenagers
in school uniforms.

So I guess I don't like it, but there are things to love
about this place, a city that wrapped me
in its arms and held on, vicelike, a bit uncomfortable
but increasingly familiar, the struggle against its grip
becoming my morning routine, as scheduled
as my bowl of cornflakes with water (milk
is an expense I can't justify) or yogurt
if I'm feeling extravagant. A local friend asked me
if I've started traveling by bus yet
and I admitted I prefer taxi, despite
her frequent warnings of rape committed
against women traveling alone and kidnappings
of tourists which are all too common after dark.
Buses run their own risks. Pickpockets, no seatbelts,
taking curves in the mountains
at 70 kilometers per hour.

"I was afraid for you to get a tattoo here,"
one roommate laughed after admiring my new ink.
"I sound ignorant." But everything is a little
dangerous here. Not more dangerous
than anywhere else, but less concealed.
I don't blame her. And I don't blame myself
for feeling alone because my blond curls stick out
in a sea of black hair and brown skin.
Vendors quickly switch to English as soon
as I approach. And *that* I do hold against them.
I don't know why. It's not their fault I don't fit here.
Because I didn't fit in Sacramento either. Boston.
Rochester. Newark. Atlanta. What I want more
than anything is a home, and it's the one thing I can't
seem to find.

Love

Whenever I want to write about love, I imagine
my professor screaming at us in fiction workshop,
“Idiosyncrasies, idiosyncrasies, idiosyncrasies!”
“One adverb, maximum, per page!” “Strong nouns
and verbs!” But what if love just makes me sad?
Can I dig deeper?

Falling in love is like missing the last step
of a short staircase. Love is like drowning
in a ball pit at Chuck E. Cheese. You’re in
no real danger, but you can’t breathe,
your arms are heavy, your heart is pounding,
and you want to cry (everyone says you should be
having a great time, so you try to smile,
but we all know it’s a grimace).

When I got divorced, I had to figure out
what to do with three bedrooms and two bathrooms.
First, I had a green room. I bought several wire
plant displays with pots in every color, an organic bag
of mulch the store clerk recommended with a smirk,
and seeds of flowers that promised to lure butterflies
and hummingbirds if I left a window open.

I planted the seeds, watered with precision,
and waited. Nothing happened. Then, I considered
a ball pit. Amazon has balls in bulk. 400 balls for $50.
A friend calculated that I would need about 30 bags
of 400. For only $1500, I could make
my dreams come true. In the end, I decided
my credit card balance was high enough already.
Sometimes when you get divorced at 26, you have to
put groceries on your MasterCard.

But love is like drowning in a ball pit
at Chuck E. Cheese. I think I'm going to stick
with that simile. Or maybe it's just like trying to fill
your house with things to replace the person that left.
I bought a hammock, a fire pit, a futon,
another television, a writing desk, an ottoman,
and all the pizza and burritos I could get my hands on.
I also sold my treadmill because who needs
to exercise when you're drowning?
Because I'm in love again and it still feels like the
bottom of a ball pit.

The kids on the outside want to be in here with me,
but they don't know that there's no air.
I'm at the point where I've stopped struggling,
resigned to laying still until someone jumps in,
not knowing I'm buried deep inside, knocking
the wind out of me as he hops
up and down on my diaphragm.
There was some air left after all.

Posthumous

I write my own death one day

from my sister's perspective. I place her in Boston,
in the snow, post-breakup.
She gets a phone call while painting
her bedroom purple. It's my landlord.
I've slit my wrists. They can't ship my body overseas.
Her ex helps her pack. Gets her to the airport.
She doesn't feel anything except the cold
east coast air on her face, tries to imagine summer
in South America. Can't.

I don't know what to write once she's on her way.
Even in fiction, there are no easy means of escape.
In reality, I have 28 days left in Peru. I'm restless.
I get a tattoo. I go to the cinema and watch
Hotel Transylvania dubbed in Spanish.
I trade work schedules for more free time, then stare
at the wall and dread the empty hours ahead.
672 of them.

I make a budget. I break it. I plan a trip to D.C.
that I can't afford. Brewery tours, expensive coffee
with leaves of foam, the espionage museum.
All I really want to do is nap next to you
for three days. I remember arriving in June,
struggling to breathe at 7,600 feet, in awe
of the llamas, the dramatic volcano backdrop,
the valiant pedestrians crossing the street
during rush hour. Now, I keep my head down,
watching for potholes, dog shit, broken glass.
671 hours.

I thought that my fictionalized sister could have

a better time in Peru than I did. She would appreciate
the food, the poverty, the history. She would reflect
on consumerism, on past relationships, on what
one can learn from loneliness. All I've discovered
is the honey pollo bacon sandwich down the street.
"Salsa?" *Solo mayonesa*.

My students laugh at the way I say *mango*,
and make jokes about the cat meat hidden
in the chifa. They love *Titanic* and *Iron Man*
and saying "fuck," which I allow because they say it
in English. They can't point me in the direction
of a good Mexican restaurant but have a lot
of cevicheria recommendations. They ask
if all Americans are left-handed.

Just me.

Bus

I'm waiting to cross the street.
A bus slows to a roll two inches
from my face and the ayudante
tosses a man out of the side door.
The driver picks up speed
just before the light turns red,
only inciting two or three angry honks
from the cars behind him
that had to brake at
the unexpected drop-off.

22

Marriage at 22 was my legacy, just like my mom,
just like my grandma. I learned this at my bridal
shower, surrounded by aunts in a timeshare suite
in Oceanside, California. They wrote advice
on napkins for me and made me read it aloud.

"Don't go to bed angry." "Marry your best friend."
"Have more than one child." Someone had dragged
a baby along and passed it to me. The crowd laughed

as I held her in front of me like a bag of dirty laundry.
They snapped pictures of my face, wrinkled
in the usual humorous disgust of a person who hates
children but has them thrust upon her
for the amusement of others.

This was my first trip to California, but I was quickly
learning that January didn't mean winter here.
I squinted against the sun shining in through

the window, reflecting off the all-white furniture
as if to highlight the big day tomorrow. "You're tall,"
he said to me when we first met in the parking lot
of Panera Bread before pulling me into a muffled hug.
He was 6'3", eight inches taller than me.

Six weeks later, we were engaged.

Nostalgia

I have 13 days left. I just pulled an ant
out of my tea, but I may even miss that a little,
the grit of the first city I discovered
on my own in over a decade.
When you're about to leave someplace,

even the most mundane details become poignant.
This is the street where I jumped over a pile of corn
on a morning run. Here is the stretch where they sell
guitars and ukuleles. I play neither.
I remember when I discovered this bridge,

the quiet one without the buses. A revelation.
The unobstructed view of Chachani without exhaust
blowing in my face. I never bought the weird fruit
from that lady on the corner, but it was comforting
to see her every day regardless.

Life after

My bed is cold. My whole house is cold, but my bed especially. I still curl up on the left side, leaving most of it empty, the cold pressing against me. Heavy. The only spots that aren't cold are the windowsills, yellow with sun, speckled black with little gnat bodies. I don't know if the gnats seek warmth, fresh air, or are searching for lost brothers and sisters. They find their kin but perish in the process. I can't clean them up, out of either reverence or disrespect. I can't tell the difference anymore. I cut off all my hair. I am both Samson and Delilah. He didn't like my hair short. He didn't want to fuck me anymore but fucked me out of obligation so I wouldn't ask him what was wrong. Because what was wrong was that he hated me. Every time I leave the house, I buy a bottle of nail polish. Then I come home to paint. It ensures I have something to do, something besides feel cold. A few hours later I pick it all off. Then I leave the house. Cash. Paint. Repeat. This pattern continues for at least two months. Maybe six. And then I feel human. A little.

Ants

I have cigarette burns on my brain.
My therapist suggested I have Intermittent
Explosive Disorder but it's just these
puckered scars, revealing themselves in bursts.

A year and a half later and I still feel numb.
Maybe that's better than the alternative.
I get up early to prune. My lease doesn't allow
pruning but I've always been a rebel.

I don't know if I do more harm than good,
if I cut away viable branches, if I tear
at the bark too fervently. I search for over an hour
for branches with no leaves, snaking their way

through the flora towards the sun, reaching
but never taking in the nutritious rays.
Now, they're in my garbage bin
and the tree is top heavy, Jessica Rabbit.

Next, I tackle the ants at the foundation
of the house. I start raking away dead leaves
and discover them: a frantic, moving carpet,
pulsing across the concrete.

Fake online therapist

I started seeing a fake online therapist,
but I think I did it to have something to write about.
The startup bros that designed this app
would surely take offense to the idea.

They would remind me they don't advertise
themselves as therapists, merely life coaches.
For $12 a week. The real online therapists
were too expensive on my $5/hour salary.

The fake online therapist doesn't use a name,
repeats everything I say back to me. They tell me
I write beautifully when I describe myself with words
like "vagabond." They remind me that life

in a new country is an adjustment, and it's okay
if I start crying over $3 avocado toast
on my day off. They tell me to keep a journal
of my feelings.

They send me heart emojis and say I can
message them next time I'm in a restaurant, sitting
across from no one. This makes my situation seem
that much more desperate, but I don't tell them.

Don't want to hurt their feelings. I've figured out
the Pizza Hut website in Spanish. There is no limit
to the amount of familia de pepperoni I can order.
That's the only thing I've learned from life in Peru.

Allergy

My friend is allergic to bones.
His body, always covered in hives,
tries to expel his insides every day.
Sitting on the couch, he will often wince
and look down at his arm, at white pressing
against the inside of his skin, stretching
unnaturally but never breaking.

If I stare at his face long enough, it changes,
the cheekbones becoming more prominent, alien,
the eyebrow line expanding and contracting,
changing his expression. At first,
the changes are subtle—I begin to wonder
why he's so angry at the joke I just told—
then, he looks like a stranger. Then, a monster.

His closet is full of shoes organized by size.
He never knows what shape his feet will be in
when he wakes up. When he wears sandals,
I can watch (though I try not to) the five prongs
of his toes pulsing like a starfish. Sometimes,
he will wobble next to me, sigh, grab
onto my shoulder, steady himself.

He told me his lungs are larger than average,
with no secure ribcage in place to contain them.
His voice booms across rooms, parking lots,
crowded city streets with no trouble at all.
I'm never lost with him around, those thundering
vibrations comfort me in their consistency,
the consistent way my ears ache when he's near.

Safe

"Have you thought about what happens if you die
over there?" my best friend asks. "Who will claim
your body?" Back from a recent stint as a teacher
in Peru, I'm heading back out to Costa Rica
in two short weeks. I can't stand being here.
It's like living in the Matrix.

I shrug. She doesn't know I often contemplate
this very topic. Six months earlier, I found myself
on an abandoned street in Arequipa with a taxi driver
who didn't speak English. It was 7 a.m.
We were both slapping our hands against the giant
wooden door of a hostel, and no one was answering.

I didn't have cell phone service yet. My Spanish
was too embarrassing to use, even in this
somewhat dire situation. Finally, after 10 minutes
of angry mutterings by him and apologetic glances
from me, the door opened. A bleary-eyed tenant
let me in, and I waved gratefully to the driver
as he got back in his car. I didn't have any money
to tip him. He could have left me on that street
with everything I owned, but he stayed by my side,
an unexpected act of kindness.

My best friend took me for my first pampering
on Saturday. The woman soaked my feet
in warm water, scrubbed them raw
with a suspicious sponge, clipped and filed my nails,
and massaged my calves as I avoided
making eye contact. She painted my toes
a shade of orange called "Sunshine State of Mind."

I don't like being touched.

That's a lie. The warmth of a friend's legs next to me
on the couch is the safest feeling I've ever had.
A boyfriend's thumb stroke, back and forth against
my wrist, is better than any orgasm.
But the brusque, disconnected hands
of the nail technician whose name I didn't know?
I won't pursue that feeling again.

Las hormigas

I've written about them before,
a carpet pulsing in the dirt.
They didn't seem so formidable
in California against the dry,
desert ground. They offered softness,
a relief to the sharp stillness
of that August afternoon in Sacramento,
too hot for the hummingbirds,
heat smothering my neighbor's stilted laughter.
The sky was so blue,
almost white against rolling yellow hills,
where no cows chewed their cud.

Here, las hormigas are their own life form,
an entire body acting individually,
and then, horrifyingly, as one.
I step on an anthill on a remote corner
of the mountain and they spring to action,
a thousand pinpricks of fire that linger
(they still linger; I don't know how long
they will linger). Back in my room that night,
they continue to scurry across my desk,
down the legs of my only chair,
through the sheets of my bed,
along my calves (which twitch, involuntary,
anticipating pain so that it's worse
when it comes).

Even when I manage to dodge las hormigas,
the pain always comes. In bursts.
A man at the hostel has your shoulders.
Another leans his head against his girlfriend's
the same way you used to against mine.
Still another sighs like you do when he's too full.

Whenever I see something new,
I want to send you a picture (a turquoise bird
a puddle full of tadpoles, a lizard the size
of my fingernail). Small things that are not new
to me anymore, but I can’t share them with you,
and they are that much smaller.

Mosquitos

I don't have to drink from you, but I can't stop.
Fruits and juices would suffice. Nectar would be
just fine. And yet. I draw my head back
and your skin is covered in red dots, swelling
against my saliva, a chemical reaction
your body can't help and one I've stopped fighting.
Leaving a little bit of me in you is horrifying
but the satisfaction is real, to know that part of you
craves it. The itch. The impending welt.
Days of discomfort, waiting for me to fade,
just to reimpose. In the wild, there are others.
Lacking. Their bodies don't provide the sustenance
I need to survive; less complexity, less crispness,
less crease between their eyebrows
when they're doing an impression. No one desecrates
pasta by rinsing it like you do. No one cringes
from water hotter than lukewarm. No one sings along
to the radio on a higher key, lets me kiss their nose
as many times as I want, suggests
"The Little Mermaid" on the third date, rests
their hands on my hips like he's holding eggs.

I've become nocturnal. Thoughts of you make
my eyes throb, from thirst or desire, I'm not sure
which. What I know for sure is that I won't make it
out here on my own. We're social creatures,
mosquitos, bothering all species with our need.
Killing millions every year without being quenched.
But your flavor is the one I can't forget.
My proboscis seeks you out, quivering every night,
my belly insatiable, able to hold three times my weight
with just you; your heat, the quiver of your breath
when I land, the goosebumps on your brown skin. I
could fight it, but I know I won't.

La lluvia

I pretend I've developed a sixth sense for the rain.
It's easy enough to do here, where the earth feels
so close. I'm encouraged to perform my duties
sin zapatos and achieve the feat by day five.
They joke by day 30 I'll be sleeping in the trees.
"With a machete," I add.

I am obsessed with the machete. I can't appreciate
enough the smooth way it removes thorns
from bamboo, with a single stroke after enough
practice. One afternoon, I slip and grab hold
of a trunk, only to be met with skin prickling
under my fingers in place of bark, a thousand
thread-thin barbs digging deeper as the days go on.

In room five, no air circulates. The tin roof thunders
during every storm from the force of pelting water.
A man with a bird's head wanders by my window
every now and then even though I'm alone on the
third floor. I think it's a ground dove

but in this poor lighting, I can't tell for sure. I wonder
where his mate is. There is never one without
the other, the red without the grey. Just seeing him,
I know she's not far behind. I can practically hear her
rustling in the brush just out of sight. It's enough
to keep me up, unblinking, waiting for her silhouette.
It doesn't come. Another sleepless night.

Bite

My ear has swollen to twice its size, but the world
is muffled. A baby hummingbird, still molting, perches
on a wire fence, watches me water the tomatoes.
It is the size of a grape. Its beak opens and closes,
but all I hear is the faintest squeak.

It's too young to know it shouldn't look at me.
Shouldn't speak to me. The mom swoops in
and chases it away, turning her long tongue to me
in scolding. I can feel her anger vibrating through
the morning air but no sound can penetrate the pus.

I take out my earrings, hoping the holes will act
as a drain, squeeze the red skin like a balloon I want
to pop. Nothing. A bit more pain. A touch of irritation.

A stray puppy wanders onto the property. I name him
Jack, after *Titanic*. I can tell he's an artist
and a romantic. We only have arroz and frijoles
to feed him so I buy a bag of puppy food
at the supermarket in town.

By the time I'm back, he's wandered on. I thought
from the tears in his eyes, the way he jumped
on my lap when I fed him, the way he followed me
into the garden and barked at the hose, I thought
that he would stick around,

that he had some unconditional love
to spread to those of us in need.

Farm work

I've regressed. I squeeze a blister
between my thumb and index finger,
hold my breath, wait for the pop
of clear liquid. Sometimes just a tear,
sometimes a small pool that drips
down my wrist, wetting my sleeve
just enough to be uncomfortable.
This I do again and again,
until my arm is covered
in welts redder than when I started.

Our host's voice is so unlike yours,
but the tone is the same. The way
her eyebrows make an unapproving "v"
in the middle of her forehead.
The deep frown, all the way down
to her chin, so deep it's a wonder
it can recover, deep enough to drown
me. Eyes wide and wild,
like she's never seen
anything as stupid as me.

Such a familiar look, it'd be comforting
if it was facing elsewhere. I turn my head
and let out one silent sob, squeeze
my eyes as briefly as I can
before getting back to work.
Later, the floor is covered
in cockroach legs snap, crackling
as I walk to the bathroom to rinse off
the day's dirt in a cold shower.
All the showers here are cold.

All the nights are loud.

Polly

I've fallen in love with a chicken in Argentina.
She is a hybrid, my host explains,
and the other chickens have rejected her.

At first, we keep her in the supply closet, away
from the others so they can't hurt her. I visit her every
morning and before bed, try to coo familiar noises.

But eventually, my host decides she has to join
the flock. Chicken bullying is so serious
that she takes refuge in Flaco's shadow

when we let them out to peck at grass and grain
in the yard, a dog who took several snaps at her
neck just this morning.

Three days later, I discover her frozen body
in the coop. It dropped down to 20 degrees
the night before. The flock refused to let her sleep

with them for warmth, preferring to watch her die
slow, cold. Alone.

Flaco

Flaco grins his toothy, gap-filled grin at me,
rolls onto his back like animals are wont to do
in the sun, bits of grass clinging to his glossy gold
and black coat. “Does he ever attack the chickens?”
I ask. “Yes,” says my host with a shrug.
“Sometimes, I hit him.”

When I first arrived, my host warned me about Flaco,
“El es un perro malo. He’s bitten four or five guys.”
An adopted street dog, Flaco warms to me
immediately and starts running with me
in the morning. Still dark at 7 a.m., his eyes glow
green in the light of my headlamp

20 or 30 feet ahead, indicating that I’m still on
the dirt road towards Rodeo. I can see my breath,
in and out in metered bursts. Trying to count them,
I lose track after a couple hundred. When I get back,
my hands, stiff, red, and cracked from cold,
burn under the lukewarm sprinkle of my shower.

I fill the tank with water from my sink and heat it
with a switch on the wall. “Don’t forget to turn
the switch off before you get in,” my host warns again
and again. He’s only been electrocuted twice
while doing renovations on his house. Maybe
there are no electricians in Las Flores, or maybe

he’s as stingy with his utilities as he is
with his condiments. He won’t buy butter,
no matter how nonchalantly I ask. I came here
to make beer, but so far all I’ve tasted is paint
for four long weeks, chalky and acrylic as it drips
into my mouth from the ceiling.

The closest place to buy beer ingredients
is two hours away. His mom keeps promising
to bring them and then cancelling.

Picnic

I make a friend at my hostel. On a hike, he stops
to rest, lights the smallest joint I've ever seen,
and offers it to me. I decline. As he inhales, I look up.
Layers of gray ice and debris hover above me.
Glaciers on Instagram are blue. I pull my phone out
to take a picture but the battery is dead from the cold.

We're in the mouth of Vinciguerra Glacier.
Every few seconds, a sharp crack makes us jump
and we stare at each other, wide-eyed, half grinning,
make jokes about the number of deaths caused
by global warming every day. "At least it would be
instant," I shrug and shiver. "And crushed by a glacier
is one of the coolest ways to go."

He sets the joint down on the ground where
it immediately blends in with rock and snow.
"Don't let me forget this," he laughs and pulls
a ham sandwich out of his backpack.
"Do you want some lunch?" "Maybe later."
My teeth won't stop chattering. My winter jacket,
a loaner from a roommate in Peru, has soaked
through to my skin.

I was not prepared to come to The End of the World,
but I'm here anyway, a 30-minute motorcycle ride
outside Ushuaia. My first, and helmetless, sure I was
going to die at every curve, my stomach plummeting
to my toes, my tongue curling up in my mouth
against a scream. "Let me breathe," my friend grunted
as I squeezed my arms around his ribs,

my grip never tight enough. He doesn't know
I wanted to kiss him the first time I saw him.

That first night in the bar, his arm around my shoulder
and head close so we could talk above the crowd,
I fought the urge to lean in, rub my face against his.
I still miss the warmth of other people.

Consejo

"You need more men in your life,"
says my host's friend, with the caveat that he
doesn't know me that well. We just met today,
at the kitchen table. He's visiting from Cosquin.

My host puts *Casper* on Netflix for his kids
and heats up some salchis in the oven,
wrapped in empanada dough.
The friend wants to know what I'm doing here,

eyes widening when he finds out
I'm divorced. That I've been divorced
for three years. "My twenties were taken up
by my husband."

I crave his attention, his fluent English.
I have barely spoken in weeks
and am forgetting every idiom, words for tools
I don't use every day, names of friends.

Spanish was supposed to replace English.
I was supposed to descend the Andes in 20 years,
wise and fully immersed. Instead, my mother
tongue is being replaced with open spaces.

Gretel Ehrlich found solace here, in the deep
valleys, the livestock, the stoic neighbors.
All I'm finding is a desire to run home. I miss
capitalism. I miss cool whip and pop tarts.

"You shouldn't be so strict with yourself."
He has green eyes, but I like him anyway.
He hugs me goodbye, says maybe we can
hang out tomorrow.

We never see each other again.
Nomad life is packed with missed
connections and dirty
laundry.

Surgery

I spent most of French class dissecting my pens
and markers. Carefully twisting off the cap,
then the bottom, the ink dripping out, staining
my binder and my fingers. It required precision
and focus. If Madam called on me, I couldn't answer.
But my pen case was full of empty shells
by the end of the period. One of the popular boys
laughed and shook his head. He found my quirks
charming while everyone else rolled their eyes.
My mom never asked why I always needed more
school supplies.

Cover art by Larry Arasin

www.ingramcontent.com/pod-product-compliance
Lightning Source LLC
LaVergne TN
LVHW050330160826
845677LV00014B/3572

* 9 7 9 8 3 5 1 1 0 8 0 0 1 *

ISBN 9798351108001
90000
9 798351 108001

Revival Poetry and Songs

Pastor Kinuthia . f. c